To:

From:

Editing by: Alice Patenaude

Photo Credits
Cover: Janna Bantan/Shutterstock
Internals: page 3, Janna Bantan/Shutterstock; page 8, Leah Zawadzki/Leah Zawadzki Photography; page 13, Leah Zawadzki/Leah Zawadzki Photography; pages 14–15, Natalia Kirichenko/Shutterstock; page 16, Leah Zawadzki/Leah Zawadzki Photography; page 21, Gina Shuppert/Gina Miller Photography; pages 22–23, Jessica Kettle/Jessica Kettle Photography; page 24, Leah Zawadzki/Leah Zawadzki Photography; page 29, Gina Shuppert/Gina Miller Photography; pages 30–31, dotshock/Shutterstock; page 32, Dmitry Naumov/Shutterstock; page 35, Jaime Lackey/Jaime Lackey Photography; pages 36–37, Rachel Vanoven/Rachel Vanoven Photography; page 38, Wes Craft/Wes Craft Photography; page 43, Soozie Harrison/Photography by Soozie; page 44, Kolett/Shutterstock; page 49, Gina Shuppert/Gina Miller Photography; pages 50–51, Pinkyone/Shutterstock; page 52, Warren Goldswain/Shutterstock; page 57, Sarah Martin/Sarah Martin Photography; pages 58–59, Sarah Martin/Sarah Martin Photography; page 60, Leah Zawadzki/Leah Zawadzki Photography; page 65, Jessica Kettle/Jessica Kettle Photography; pages 66–67, altanaka/Shutterstock; page 68, Mary Schannen/Mélange Photography; page 71, Janna Bantan/Shutterstock; pages 72–73, Gina Shuppert/Gina Miller Photography; page 74, Valerie Baillargeon/COLIBRIPHOTO; page 79, Sarah Martin/Sarah Martin Photography; pages 80–81, Sarah Martin/Sarah Martin Photography; page 82, ParkerDeen/Getty Images; page 87, Natalia Kirichenko/Shutterstock; pages 88–89, Jaime Lackey/Jaime Lackey Photography; page 90, wavebreakmedia/Shutterstock; page 95, Sarah Martin/Sarah Martin Photography; pages 96–97, lostinbids/iStock; page 98, Gina Shuppert/Gina Miller Photography; page 103, Monkey Business Images/Shutterstock; pages 104–105, vgm/Shutterstock; page 106, Soozie Harrison/Photography by Soozie; page 111, Soozie Harrison/Photography by Soozie; pages 112–113, Valerie Baillargeon/COLIBRIPHOTO; page 114, Mary Schannen/Mélange Photography; page 119, Sundari/Shutterstock; pages 120–121, Leah Zawadzki/Leah Zawadzki Photography; page 126, Wes Craft/Wes Craft Photography; page 128, Sunny studio/Shutterstock

Published by Simple Truths, an imprint of Sourcebooks, Inc.
P.O. Box 4410, Naperville, Illinois 60567-4410
(630) 961-3900
Fax: (630) 961-2168
www.sourcebooks.com

Printed and bound in China.
OGP 10 9 8 7 6 5 4 3 2

To watch an inspirational movie from **this** book along with more than 50 other uplifting movies, please visit *www.simpletruthsmovies.com*

If you would like to receive the movie for this book in an immediate digital download or DVD, please contact us at **1-800-900-3427**

• Vicki Reece •

THE Joy OF MOM

Celebrating a mother's love

simple truths®
Your Destination For Inspiration

an imprint of Sourcebooks, Inc.

Introduction

How do you encapsulate the joy, honor, gift, and privilege of being a mom? It's in the moments. The tiny, indelibly precious, delicious, almost indescribable moments. From the second we hear, feel, and see our child's first heartbeat to experiencing their first breath, becoming a mom is truly understanding Elizabeth Stone's quote for the first time:

"Making the decision to have a child...is to decide forever to have your heart go walking around outside your body."

As a mom, you can watch your children silently sleeping for hours on end and feel sheer joy for every tiny move they make. Their "firsts" are your "firsts"—their first steps, the first day at school, the first time the school bus pulls away, or when we let go of the back of their bicycle. Their first crush, date, or heartbreak. Taking them to college or walking them down the aisle. All their firsts not only take our breath away, but also leave our hearts right there with them.

I've been collecting, curating, and crafting quotes for as long as I can remember. Compiled into worn journals, my favorite words of inspiration have helped me through some pretty rough days.

There is such soul, grace, and love in everything we do as moms, every single day…and every precious and sacred moment in them. It's the soul of who we are and the fabric of our lives—one that will never know compromise. And some days when we're exhausted and at our wit's end, we feel like we have no more to give. That's when, as moms, we give even more—lovingly, gratefully, and with all our heart.

The "love affair" with our children begins the second we begin our new roles as moms:

From the second that I found out that I was cradling you in my womb, I'd have given my life for you. I could feel you grow, feel you move, and feel you kick. The sound of your heartbeat was the most perfect sound I had ever heard. Our bond grew every day. My hand instinctively rested on my belly to protect you, as I counted down the days until I could hold you in my arms. Even through the unspeakable pain of labor, my only concern was your safety. Then you arrived and were more beautiful and perfect than I could have ever imagined. And I finally knew what love was, unconditional love. It was a love so strong that it overwhelmed me. There was nothing

I would not do for you. You were my first priority, my reason for being, my child. You still continue to grow, but those feelings do not fade. So please understand that I will worry, at times you will think me overprotective and expect me to realize you are "growing up." Because no matter how big you grow, I will always see my child, my baby. My instinct will always be to protect you, and I will always love you more than you will ever know. Because I am your mom and you will always be my child.

~Steph Turner

I hope the quotes and images in *The Joy of Mom* touch, move, and inspire you too. Enjoy!

If I could give you one thing in life,
I would give you the ability to see yourself
through my eyes. Only then would you
realize how special you are to me.

Unknown

Give the ones you love wings

to fly, roots to come back,

and reasons to stay.

♥ DALAI LAMA XIV ♥

My sweet child, you are the light in my eyes,

the beat of my heart, the whisper in

my soul. You inspire me, always.

More than you could ever know.

♥ VICKI REECE ♥

THE *Joy* OF MOM

You'll fly away,
but take my hand until that day.

So when they ask how far love goes,
When my job's done you'll
be the one who knows.

Dar Williams

Prepare the
child for the path,
not the path
for the child.

UNKNOWN

Sometimes when I need a miracle
I look into my daughter's eyes and
realize I've already created one.

Unknown

A baby asked God, "They tell me you are sending me to earth tomorrow, but how am I going to live there being so small and helpless?" God said, "Your angel will be waiting for you and will take care of you."

The baby asked, "Who will protect me?"

God said, "Your angel will defend you

even if it means risking her life."

The baby said, "God, if I am to leave now,

please tell me my angel's name." God said,

you will simply call her 'Mom.'"

♥ UNKNOWN ♥

I will nurture, protect, guide, and love you more deeply than you could ever imagine. From your first heartbeat till my very last.

Vicki Reece

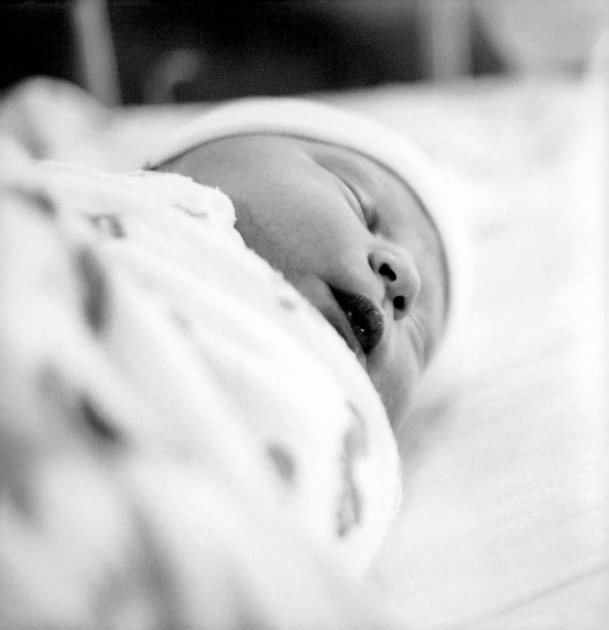

The best
security blanket a child
can have is parents who
respect each other.

JANE BLAUSTONE

In my daughter's eyes, I am a hero.
I am strong and wise, and I know no fear.
But the truth is plain to see:
She was sent to rescue me.
I see who I want to be
In my daughter's eyes.

Martina McBride

Behind all your stories is

always your mother's story.

Because hers is where yours begin.

♥ MITCH ALBOM ♥

Mom, thank you for
always being there for me.
Not just when I needed you,
but for when I needed you most.

♥ VICKI REECE ♥

When the winds blow, which they will,
may our children always stand strong
and steady in who they are,
and in all they believe in.

Vicki Reece

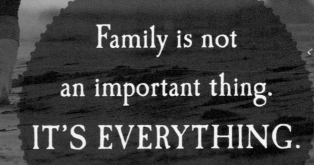

Family is not
an important thing.
IT'S EVERYTHING.

MICHAEL J. FOX

You have my whole heart for my whole life.

Vicki Reece

A mother understands what
a child does not say.

Jewish Proverb

There are only 940 Saturdays between your child's birth and them leaving for college.

DR. HARLEY ROTBART

A mom is a daughter's "first" friend.
And, through life, becomes
her "best" friend.

Vicki Reece

Children are love made visible.

♥ AMERICAN PROVERB ♥

Being a mom is simply the highest calling.

♥ VICKI REECE ♥

"Sometimes," said Pooh,
"the smallest things take up the
most room in your heart."

A. A. Milne

When a child gives you a gift, even if it is
a rock they just picked up, exude gratitude.
It might be the only thing they have to give,
and they have chosen to give it to you.

Dean Jackson

When the grass-stained knees have come and gone,

No handprints on the wall,

You'll miss the things you washed away

When your children are not small.

Now you long for peaceful nights.

You pray for sleep, for calm.

Yet soon you're going to miss this chance

To hold your child in your arms.

"One minute, son, I'm washing up.

I promise I won't be long."

You forget you've a lifetime of pots to clean,

But your children aren't children for long.

So no matter how busy you think you are,

Always make time for a kiss.

And try to appreciate the small things,

For they'll be the things that you'll miss.

♥ STEPH TURNER ♥

I want to be a mom that
my girls look at and say,
"I want to be like her."

Unknown

Enjoy the little things,
for one day you may look
back and realize they
were the big things.

ROBERT BRAULT

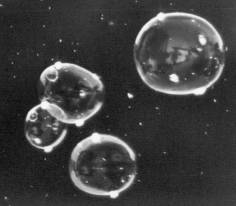

How would you nurture her if you
were the mother of little you?

Kris Carr

If I had to choose between

breathing and loving my children,

I would use my last breath

to tell them "I love you."

♥ UNKNOWN ♥

I carried you inside me for nine months,

and in my heart forever…

♥ VICKI REECE ♥

Children will not remember you for the material things you provided but for the feeling that you cherished them.

Richard L. Evans

Always kiss your children good night, even if they're already asleep.

H. JACKSON BROWN JR.

Before you were born I carried you under my heart. From the moment you arrived in this world until the moment I leave it, I will always carry you in my heart.

Mandy Harrison

A mom's hug lasts long after she lets go.

♥ UNKNOWN ♥

Every mom has a mission.

To love, guide, and protect her family.

Don't mess with her while she's on it.

♥ VICKI REECE ♥

Being a mother is learning about strengths
you didn't know you had, and dealing
with fears you didn't know existed.

Linda Wooten

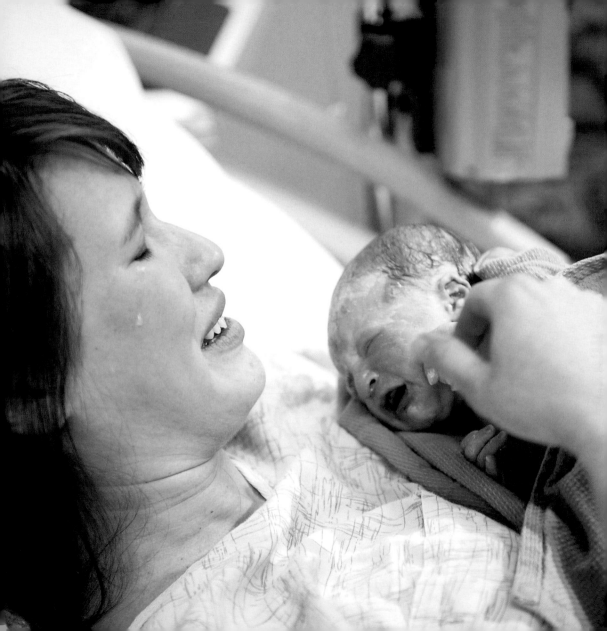

The key to my heart?

My children.

UNKNOWN

While we teach and inspire our children, it's they who "truly" teach and inspire us. Every day.

Vicki Reece

Mostly I wish you joy.
Joy is the most important thing in life.
Wherever it can be found.

Unknown

There are
some moments
that will stay
with us forever.

VICKI REECE

If you have a mom, there is nowhere
you are likely to go where a prayer
has not already been.

Robert Brault

No matter how big you get.
No matter where your journey in life takes you. You'll always be my little boy. And I'll always be here for you, beside you…or behind you.

♥ VICKI REECE ♥

A happy child has a joyful mother.

♥ WANDA E. BRUNSTETTER ♥

I never knew how much I loved your father
until I saw how much he loved you.

Unknown

Four very
powerful words to
say to your child:
I believe in you.

KEVIN HEATH

Simple moments are among the most precious. Cherish them, for time passes much too quickly.

Vicki Reece

i carry your heart with me

(i carry it in my heart)

♥ E. E. CUMMINGS ♥

There's no way to be a perfect mother and a
million ways to be a good one.

♥ JILL CHURCHILL ♥

If it were possible to go back to when my children were young... For a day. For an hour. Even for five minutes. What I would give to be able to.

Vicki Reece

A mommy's job
means getting paid
with hugs and kisses.

UNKNOWN

THE *Joy* OF MOM

You will never have this day with your children again.

Tomorrow, they'll be a little older
than they were today.

This day is a gift.

Breathe and notice.

Smell and touch them; study their faces
and little feet and pay attention.

Relish the charms of the present.

Enjoy today, Mama.

It will be over before you know it.

Jen Hatmaker

There is no love or devotion like
that of a mother for her child.

♥ VICKI REECE ♥

A mother's arms are made
of tenderness and children
sleep soundly in them.

♥ VICTOR HUGO ♥

Before I was a Mom...
I never knew that something so small could affect my life so much. I never knew I would cherish every moment and those moments would turn into memories that would last forever. I never felt my heart break into a million pieces when I couldn't stop the hurt. I never knew my heart could love this much.

Unknown

Children are
made readers on the laps
of their parents.

EMILIE BUCHWALD

You never understand life
until it grows inside of you.

Sandra Chami Kassis

People who say

they sleep like a baby

usually don't have one.

♥ LEO J. BURKE ♥

Until you've…counted little fingers, counted little toes, held a little hand, kissed a little nose, soothed a little tummy, read to little ears, powdered a little booty, wiped away little tears, you haven't known love.

♥ UNKNOWN ♥

Don't talk to me right now...
I was up all night keeping my parents
awake and I'm exhausted.

Unknown

No symphony
orchestra has ever played
music like a two-year-old
child laughing with
a puppy.

BERN WILLIAMS

There are people who take the
heart out of you, and there are
those who put it back.

Elizabeth David

Be faithful in small things
because it is in them that
your strength lies.

♥ MOTHER TERESA ♥

I am a mother.

Life is tough but I'm tougher.

♥ UNKNOWN ♥

A mother's love for her child is like nothing else in the world. It's fierce, forever, and will let nothing stand in its path.

Vicki Reece

A mother's lap.
The safest place on earth.

UNKNOWN

His little hands stole my heart...
and his little feet ran away with it.

Unknown

Mothers hold their children's
hands just for a little while,
but their hearts forever.

♥ IRISH PROVERB ♥

There will be so many times you feel like you've failed. But in the eyes, heart, and mind of your child you are Super Mom.

♥ STEPHANIE PRECOURT ♥

My precious child, wherever your journey in life may take you...I pray you'll always be safe, enjoy the ride, and never forget your way back home.

Vicki Reece

I'll love you forever,
I'll like you for always,
As long as I'm living,
my baby you'll be.

ROBERT MUNSCH

Conclusion

So much has happened since I embarked on my remarkable journey as a mother…and my journey to help make a difference in the lives of children and moms everywhere through Joy of Mom.

Twenty years have passed all too quickly. My children are in college and my husband and I officially became empty-nesters. I'm so not ready for this stage, but are moms ever really ready for it?

It feels so unnatural for my children to have left the nest. But I keep my perspective, knowing in my heart that the most important job we can do as moms is to raise our babies so they may one day flourish on their own and be happy, confident, capable, compassionate, contributing young adults.

When that time comes, moms come to fully understand Dorothy Fisher's quote:

> "A mother is not a person to lean on, but a person to make leaning unnecessary."

No matter how often we hear it, time IS really precious. What I wouldn't give to be able to press that Replay button…even for a moment! The love, lessons, and life experiences we shared with our children will stay with them forever. And they will pass on our love and legacy.

I hope you enjoyed all the words and images in *The Joy of Mom* as much as I did!

My advice?

Take in every precious moment to its fullest.

Walk in gratitude every step along the greatest, most sacred, and special journey we'll ever travel…motherhood. As I always say, "Love is in the details." And the details are life.

"You are a miracle.

And I have to love you this fiercely: So that you can feel it even after you leave for school, or even while you are asleep, or even after your childhood becomes a memory.

You'll forget all this when you grow up. But it's okay.

Being a mother means having your heart broken.

And it means loving and losing and falling apart and coming back together.

And it's the best there is. And also, sometimes, the worst.

Sometimes you won't have anyone to talk to.

Sometimes you'll wonder if you've forgotten who you are.

But you must remember this: What you're doing matters.

And you have to be brave with your life so that others can be brave with theirs.

The truth is, being a woman is a gift.

Tenderness is a gift.

Intimacy is a gift.

And nurturing the good in this world is nothing short of a privilege.

That's why I have to love you this way. So I can give what I have to you. So that you can carry it in your body and pass it on.

I have watched you sleep. I've kissed you a million times. And I know something that you don't, yet:

You are writing the story of your ONLY life every single minute of every day.

And my greatest hope for you, sweet child, is that I can teach you how to write a good one."

—Katherine Center

About the Author

The mom of three children and three furry babies, Vicki Reece is a former ad executive who left it all behind to make positive multimedia products for children and families. When her children were small, Vicki became upset by the violent and negative toys and messages marketed to children. Not one to sit on the sidelines, she began producing children's music, videos, and games that were positive and sent love-filled messages. Her first children's computer software game, *Jack's House*, was warmly received and was followed by *Jack's Attic*.

Moms and children loved her products. They told their friends who told their friends. It went viral, the good old-fashioned way. Passionate moms rallied around her. They connected with her on the most visceral level—with the joy and journey of being a mom.

Vicki has been featured on *The View, CNN, Fox & Friends,* spotlighted in network interviews on ABC, NBC, CBS, WGN, CLTV, and showcased in articles in more than one hundred newspapers and seventy-five magazines, including *Vanity Fair, The Times,* the *Wall Street Journal,* and *Child Magazine.*

Today, Vicki's inspirational words reach and touch millions of moms and women around the world daily on Joy of Mom, a community dedicated to connecting and empowering women. *The Joy of Mom* is the culmination of Vicki's lifelong dream and journey. Join Vicki and millions of passionate women on their most miraculous and important journey, being a mom. ♥

For more information about Vicki or to connect with her, visit **www.facebook.com/joyofmom** or **www.joyofmom.com.**